Lucid Dreaming

A Comprehensive Guide To Discovering The Lucid Dream Realm And Achieving Mastery In Oneironautics

(A Concise Handbook For Acquiring The Skill Of Inducing Lucid Dream States)

Neville Fawcett

TABLE OF CONTENT

Methods For Extending The Duration Of Lucid Dreams 1

Mnemonic Induction Of Lucid Dreams) 47

Technique Of Lucid Dreaming 54

Strategies For Achieving Proficiency In Lucid Dreaming 58

Amplifying And Extending The Phenomenon Of Lucid Dreaming 71

Triumphs And Setbacks: Unlocking The Art Of Interpretation 92

Methods For Extending The Duration Of Lucid Dreams

The feeling that it is possible to control the dream is so exciting that some people can't be able to continue with the dream. Indeed, certain individuals rouse from their dream state within a matter of minutes upon the realization of being in a dream. Nevertheless, there exist various strategies through which you can assume control and extend the duration of your vision.

"You can extend the duration of a lucid dream through the utilization of the following techniques:

Please return to your slumber.

Upon rousing from a state of lucid dreaming, it is advised not to remain awake immediately and relinquish the dream. Make an effort to recollect as many particulars as you can regarding the dream. Envision yourself situated precisely at the same geographic coordinates as you were within the dream. It is also important to envision that all individuals partaking in the dream still persist. Should you succeed in returning to slumber, you shall effortlessly proceed with the continuation of the lucid dream.

The technique for extending the duration of lucid dreams is relatively straightforward, particularly if one has engaged in a few hours of sleep prior to awakening. Nevertheless, should you have already engaged in several hours of sleep, reinitiating the process may prove somewhat challenging, thereby impeding the continuation of the lucid dreaming experience.

Ensure that your cognitive faculties are vigilant.

Upon awakening, engage in an activity that stimulates cognitive function to enhance your awareness of the environment. For example, it is recommended to engage in a brief stroll within the confines of the bedroom prior to returning to a state of slumber. Additionally, you may partake in a modest meal. Throughout this duration, you will be engaging your cognitive faculties whilst sleep hormones are still present in your circulatory system. Upon resuming slumber, your cognitive faculties shall become heightened, enabling you to discern the onset of dreaming.

Perform a somersault or execute a backward tumbling motion.

Studies have indicated that individuals proficient in lucid dreaming have the capacity to extend the duration of their dreams through techniques such as rotating their dream form or executing a backward descent. This approach is suitable in situations where the individual experiencing the lucid dream possesses consciousness of its imminent conclusion. You will become aware that the lucid dream is nearing its conclusion when the clarity of structures and individuals dwindles.

▢ Vigorously rub your palms together.

Typically, individuals who experience lucid dreaming tend to awaken as a result of the exhilaration derived from realizing that they are indeed in a dream state. By engaging in the act of gently caressing your hands within the realm of your heightened dream state, you shall effectively shift your focus away from prevailing exhilaration, thereby enhancing the duration of your lucid dreaming experience. Continue doing the task until your attention shifts to another matter.

Do not attempt to immediately manipulate the dream.

Once you become aware of being in a dream and acquire the ability to manipulate all aspects of it, refrain from hastily altering the course of events. You have the opportunity to pursue the dream and observe its outcome. There is no need for you to exert effort towards altering the sequence of events. Once the excitement has subsided, it is possible to alter the course of events.

Maintain a state of calm and composure.

Upon the realization that one is experiencing a state of lucid dreaming, it is advisable to endeavor to maintain a state of utmost composure. Persuade your ideal physique that all is well, thereby negating the need for any unease regarding the unfolding circumstances. If you are able to maintain a composed demeanor, you will successfully surmount the exhilaration and thereby prevent rousing from slumber.

DREAM ANALYSIS

Perchance, we are now inclined to suspect that the analysis of dreams possesses the potential to offer us insights into the intricate workings of our psychological apparatus, an aspect that we have hitherto sought in vain from the realms of philosophy. We shall, however, deviate from this path and redirect our attention back to our initial quandary once we have elucidated the topic of dream distortion. The issue has emerged regarding the analysis of dreams containing unpleasant content as the manifestation of desires. We now understand that this is achievable in instances where there has been alteration of dreams, where the unpleasant content merely serves as a façade for the desired outcome. Given our assumptions regarding the two psychic instances, we can now assert that unpleasant dreams indeed possess a quality that is displeasing to the second instance, while simultaneously fulfilling a desire of the first instance. They can be regarded as aspirational fantasies in that every dream originates initially, whereas the subsequent occurrence only serves to resist the dream, rather than contribute to its creative development. If we confine ourselves to an examination of the contribution made by the second instance, the comprehension of the dream will forever elude us. Should we proceed in such a manner, all the enigmas that the authors have encountered within the dream would remain unresolved.

It is necessary to conduct a fresh analysis for each case in order to provide evidence that the dream in question actually bears a hidden significance, which ultimately manifests as the realization of a desire. I hereby choose several dreams characterized by distressing contents and endeavor to engage in their analysis. They are partially the fantasies of hysterical individuals, necessitating extensive introductory statements, and occasionally an analysis of the mental processes that manifest in hysteria. I am unable to, however, elude this additional challenge in the exposition.

When administering an analytic therapy to a patient with psychoneurotic tendencies, dreams consistently serve as the focal point of our discourse, as previously mentioned. Therefore, it is essential for him to receive all the appropriate psychological explanations, which have greatly contributed to my own understanding of his symptoms. In doing so, I engage in thorough criticism, which may be equally as sharp as what I anticipate from my peers. My patients consistently raise a contradiction to the thesis that all dreams are wish fulfillments. Here are several instances of the hypothetical evidence that has been provided to counter this stance.

"I have frequently observed that you consistently assert that dreams possess the capacity to materialize into reality," initiates a shrewd female patient. Now, I shall recount a dream with contrasting content, where a desire of mine is left unfulfilled. Can you elucidate how you harmonize that with your theory? The vision is as follows:

I desire to host a dinner, but unfortunately, I do not possess any ingredients except for a small quantity of smoked salmon. I contemplate the notion of going to the market, but then I recall that it is Sunday afternoon, a time when all the shops are closed. I then attempt to make telephonic contact with several caterers, however, the telephone system appears to be non-functional...

Therefore, I must withdraw my desire to host a dinner.

I respond, undoubtedly, that the interpretation of this dream can only be determined through analysis, although I concede that upon initial inspection, it appears rational and cohesive, resembling the antithesis of wish-fulfillment. I inquire as to the cause that has elicited the emergence of this dream. You are aware that the catalyst for a dream often resides within the events of the preceding day."

Analysis.— The spouse of the patient, a morally upright and scrupulous wholesale butcher, informed her the day prior that he is experiencing excessive weight gain and consequently must commence treatment for obesity. He had intentions to rise early, engage in physical activity, adhere to a disciplined dietary regimen, and most importantly, decline any further invitations to supper. She proceeds to jovially recount how her husband, while at an inn table, had made the acquaintance of an artist who insisted on painting his portrait because the painter had never encountered such an expressive visage. However, her spouse had replied in a crude manner, expressing his gratitude for the recognition but firmly asserting his belief that capturing a portion of the posterior of a youthful woman would be more appealing to the artist than depicting his entire visage. She expressed her deep affection for her husband at that time and enjoyed teasing him extensively. She had also requested him to refrain from sending her any caviar. What does that mean?

In point of fact, she had long harbored a desire to consume a caviar sandwich every morning, but had begrudged herself the expenditure. Undoubtedly, she would expeditiously obtain the caviar from her husband, promptly upon making the request. However, she had implored him not to deliver the caviar, so that she could extend the playful banter about it.

This explanation appears implausible to me. Concealed intentions often seek refuge behind these unsatisfactory explanations. We are reminded of subjects who were hypnotized by Bernheim and followed a posthypnotic order. When asked about their motives, instead of answering "I do not know why I did that," they had to create a reason that was obviously inadequate. It is highly likely that a similar situation exists with regard to the caviar of my patient. I observe that she is compelled to generate an unrealized desire in life. Her dream also reflects the fulfillment of the desire. What is the underlying reason for her desire to possess an unfulfilled wish?

The concepts that have been presented thus far are insufficient for the interpretation of the dream. I beg for more. Following a brief intermission that corresponds to the successful resolution of a resistance, she proceeds to disclose further information about her activities the day prior. Specifically, she shares that she paid a visit to an acquaintance whom she harbors feelings of jealousy towards, primarily due to the consistent praise her husband bestows upon this individual. Luckily, this acquaintance possesses a slender and lean physique, which her spouse finds attractive in individuals with a more ample stature. What did this lean friend speak of? Manifesting an inherent desire to attain a slightly greater level of plumpness. She additionally inquired of my patient, "May I inquire as to when you might extend another invitation to us?" You consistently possess an exceptionally commendable dining arrangement.

The significance of the dream has now become evident. I might inform the patient in a more formal manner: "It is as if you had contemplated, upon the moment of your request, 'Certainly, I will extend an invitation to you, so that you may indulge in abundant food in the confines of my residence and further delight my spouse.'" "I would prefer to abstain from providing any further supper." The dream subsequently informs you that you are incapable of hosting a meal, thus granting your desire to refrain from contributing to the completion of your friend's figure. The decision made by your spouse to decline dinner invitations in order to achieve weight loss offers the lesson that one gains weight from the indulgences served in social gatherings. Now, only minimal discussion is required to verify the solution. The source of the smoked salmon in the dream is yet to be identified. Could you kindly explain the manifestation of the salmon featured in the dream you mentioned?" she responded, "This acquaintance shares a strong preference for smoked salmon as a dish. I happen to be acquainted with this woman, and I can verify this by stating that she harbors the same level of resentment towards the salmon as my patient harbors towards the caviar.

The dream allows for the consideration of yet another and more precise interpretation, which is only necessitated by a subordinate circumstance. The two interpretations are not in conflict with one another; rather, they complement each other and provide a coherent example of the typical ambiguity found in dreams as well as in all other psychological phenomena. We have observed that simultaneously with her subconscious longing for the negation of the wish, the patient is in fact preoccupied with obtaining an unsatisfied desire (the caviar sandwiches). Her friend also had expressed a desire, specifically, to become heavier, and it would not be surprising if our lady had dreamt that the wish of the friend was not being realized. Because she desires that her friend's wish for weight gain not be granted. Instead of this, nevertheless, she dreams that one of her own desires remains unfulfilled. The dream becomes susceptible to a new interpretation if, in the dream, she does not intend herself but her friend. This occurs if she has placed herself in the position of her friend, or, in other words, has identified herself with her friend.

I believe that she has indeed accomplished this, and as an indication of her identification, she has manifested an unattained desire in reality. What is the significance of this excessive identification? To clarify this matter, a comprehensive exposition is imperative. Identification plays a crucial role in the mechanism of hysterical symptoms, as it allows patients to not only represent their own experiences but also the experiences of numerous other individuals. In doing so, they are able to suffer on behalf of a large group of people and effectively portray the various characters in a drama solely through their own personalities. It must be noted here that this is a widely recognized phenomenon in which individuals with hysteria are capable of replicating all the symptoms that impress them when they observe them in others, as if their empathy is stimulated to the point of reproduction.

However, this merely indicates the manner in which the psychic process is discharged through hysterical imitation; the manner in which a psychic act unfolds and the act itself are two distinct entities. The latter is somewhat more intricate than one might envision the replication of hysterical subjects to be: it corresponds to an unconscious ascertained process, as illustrated by an example. The physician, who has a female patient exhibiting a specific type of twitching, is not taken aback when he later discovers that this particular hysterical episode has been emulated by other patients sharing the same hospital room. He internally recognizes that others have observed her and have likewise succumbed to this phenomenon, which can be referred to as psychic contagion. Yes, however, psychic infection progresses in somewhat the following manner: Typically, patients possess a greater understanding of one another than the physician has of each individual, and they demonstrate concern for each other once the doctor's visit concludes. Some individuals experience an onset of distress today, when it becomes recognized by others that the source of their emotional turmoil lies in receiving a letter from their place of origin, prompting feelings of lovesickness or similar afflictions. Their sympathy is aroused, and the following syllogism, which does not reach consciousness, is completed in them: "If it is possible to experience this kind of attack from such causes, I too may experience this kind of attack, for I have the same reasons." If this were a cycle capable of becoming conscious, it would perhaps manifest itself as fear of experiencing the same attack; however, it occurs in another psychological sphere, and therefore culminates in the realization of the dreaded symptom. Identification is thus not a simple imitation, but rather a empathetic connection based on the same origin; it embodies a "as though" attitude, and alludes to a shared attribute that has persisted in the subconscious.

Identification is commonly employed in the context of hysteria to express sexual orientation. A woman prone to bouts of hysteria is most readily identifiable, though not exclusively, with individuals whom she has engaged in sexual relations with or who have had sexual intercourse with the same individuals as herself. Language encompasses this idea: two individuals in a romantic relationship are united as a single entity. This notion holds true in both the exaggerated imagination and the subconscious dream state. It suffices to consider the act of sexual intimacy for the purpose of identification, regardless of whether it is realized in reality or not. The patient, therefore, abides by the principles of the hysterical thought processes only when she manifests her jealousy towards her friend (which, in addition, she herself acknowledges to be unjustified, as she places herself in her friend's position and identifies herself with her by creating a symptom - the denied wish). I would be happy to further elucidate the process in question in the following manner: The individual in question places herself in the position of her friend within the dream, as her friend has assumed the role formerly held by her in relation to her husband, and as she desires to occupy her friend's place in her husband's esteem[2].

The contradiction to my theory about dreams in the case of another female patient, who was the most clever among all my dreamers, was resolved in a simpler manner, although according to the scheme that the failure to fulfill one wish signifies the fulfillment of another. I once elucidated to her that the dream is a desire for attainment. The following day, she recounted a dream in which she was engaged in a journey alongside her mother-in-law to their shared summer retreat. Now I am aware that she had vehemently resisted the idea of spending the summer in the vicinity of her mother-in-law. Additionally, it was evident to me that she had fortuitously evaded encountering her mother-in-law by opting to lease a luxurious property situated in a remote countryside retreat. Now, the dream has contrary to my theory of wish-fulfillment in the dream, reversed this desired solution. Is this not a blatant contradiction? Indeed, it was imperative to derive the inferences from this dream in order to ascertain its interpretation. In accordance with this dream, I found myself in error. It was thus her desire that I should be in the wrong, and this desire was portrayed as fulfilled in the dream. However, the desire for me to be in the wrong, which was fulfilled in the setting of the countryside dwelling, alluded to a more profound issue. During that period, I had firmly concluded, based on the information provided by her analysis, that a notable event must have occurred at a specific point in her life, which was significant for her illness. She had refuted it due to its absence in her recollection. We eventually reached the realization that I was correct. Her desire for me to be in the wrong, which has been transformed into a dream, aligns with the justifiable wish that those events, which were only suspected at the time, had never occurred at all.

Through inference, and based solely on a presumption, I took the liberty of interpreting a minor incident in the situation involving an acquaintance, who had been my colleague throughout the eight semesters of the Gymnasium. He once attended a lecture of mine delivered to a small gathering, on the novel topic of the dream as the realization of a desire. He returned to his residence and experienced a vivid dream in which he had undergone the misfortune of losing all his business attire, considering his occupation as a lawyer. Subsequently, he proceeded to voice his grievances regarding this matter to me. I sought solace in the evasion: "One cannot emerge victorious in every suit," yet I privately pondered: "If for eight years I occupied the position of Primus on the first bench, while he resided somewhere amidst the middle of the class, might he not naturally harbor a longing from his early days?"

Is there a chance that I may, as well, fully embarrass myself?

Similarly, I was presented with another dream of a bleaker nature by a female patient, which contradicted my theory of the wish-dream. The patient, a young girl, commenced her narrative by stating, "It is pertinent to recall that my sister currently has only one male child, Charles, as she experienced the unfortunate loss of her eldest son, Otto, during my stay at her residence." Otto was my favorite; I was the one who truly nurtured him. I am also fond of the other young gentleman, though naturally not to the same extent as the deceased individual. I had a dream last night wherein I witnessed the lifeless body of Charles before me. He was lying peacefully in his small casket, with his hands gracefully folded. Candles were placed all around, evoking a resemblance to the unforgettable period of little Otto's passing, an event that deeply affected me. Kindly elucidate the meaning behind this, if you would. Do you have knowledge of me: Am I truly immoral to desire for my sister to be deprived of her sole remaining child? Alternatively, does the dream imply that I desire for Charles to deceased instead of Otto, whom I hold in much higher regard?"

I assured her that such an interpretation was infeasible. After careful deliberation, I managed to impart to her the analysis of the dream, which she subsequently corroborated.

Due to the untimely loss of her parents, the girl was raised in the residence of her significantly older sister, where she encountered a gentleman amongst the acquaintances and visitors who left a profound and enduring impact on her heart. It appeared for a period of time that these barely expressed relationships were destined to culminate in marriage, but this joyful outcome was hindered by the actions of the sister, whose motivations have yet to be fully explained. After the intermission, the gentleman who was fondly regarded by our patient refrained from visiting the residence: she herself achieved autonomy some duration subsequent to the demise of young Otto, towards whom her sentiment had since shifted. However, her efforts to extricate herself from the attachment she had developed towards her sister's friend were unsuccessful. Her sense of pride compelled her to stay away from him; however, she found it unfeasible to transfer her affections to the other suitors who presented themselves sequentially. Whenever the gentleman whom she loved, who was a member of the literary profession, announced a lecture anywhere, she was certain to be found in the audience; she also took advantage of every other opportunity to observe him from a distance without being noticed by him. :I recalled that the day prior, she had informed me of the Professor's planned attendance at a specific concert, expressing her own intent to be present as well, for the purpose of experiencing the pleasure of his presence. This event occurred on the day of the envisioned scenario, and the musical performance was scheduled to occur on the day she informed me about the dream. I have now comprehended the accurate interpretation, and I inquired of her if she could recall any occurrence that had transpired subsequent to the demise of young Otto. She replied promptly: "Certainly; at that time, the Professor returned after a prolonged absence, and I witnessed his presence once again beside the casket of young Otto." It unfolded precisely as I had anticipated. I interpreted the dream as follows: "In the event that the other boy were to pass away, the identical occurrence would be replicated." You would spend the day with your sister, the Professor would certainly arrive in order to offer condolences, and you would encounter him again under identical circumstances as previously observed. The dream symbolizes solely this underlying desire of yours to reunite with him, against which you are internally struggling. I am aware that you are in possession of the ticket for today's concert within your bag. Your desire is characterized by impatience; it has foreseen the forthcoming encounter that is scheduled for today, several hours in advance."

In order to conceal her desire, she had evidently chosen a circumstance where such wishes are commonly repressed - a situation filled with so much sorrow that love is not considered. However, it is highly likely that even in the actual situation at the bedside of the second, more dearly loved boy, which the dream faithfully replicated, she had not been able to suppress her feelings of affection for the visitor whom she had missed for such a long period.

An alternative explanation was discovered in the case of another female patient who, in her earlier years, was distinguished by her quick wit and cheerful demeanor and who still displayed these qualities, at least in the notion that arose during her treatment.

In relation to an extended vision, it appeared to this woman that she perceived her adolescent daughter, aged fifteen, lifeless lying in a casket before her. She possessed a strong inclination to transform this dream-image into an objection to the theory of wish-fulfillment, although she herself suspected that the specific detail of the box might lead to a different conception of the dream. During the course of the analysis, it occurred to her that the previous evening's conversation among the company had revolved around the English word "box" and the various translations of it into German, such as box, theater box, chest, box on the ear, and so on. From other components of the same dream, it is now possible to ascertain that the woman had deduced the correlation between the English word "box" and the German term "Buchsë," prompting her subsequent preoccupation with the knowledge that "Buchsë" (along with "box") is employed in colloquial discourse to designate the female genital organ. It was therefore feasible, taking into account her perspectives on the topic of topographical anatomy, to infer that the child in the box symbolized a fetus in the uterus of the mother. At this juncture in the explanation, she ceased to deny the congruence between the depiction of the dream and one of her desires. Similar to numerous other young women, she was far from content when she became pregnant, and admitted to me on multiple occasions her desire for her child to perish before its birth. In a fit of rage following a traumatic altercation with her spouse, she even resorted to striking her abdomen with her fists with the intention of harming the fetus within. Therefore, the deceased child represented the actual realization of a desire, albeit a desire that had been set aside for a period of fifteen years. It is not unexpected, given the extended timeframe, that the recognition of this wish fulfillment had faded. There have been numerous alterations in the interim period.

The particular group of dreams, of which the last two mentioned are a part, centering around the distressing theme of the death of loved ones, will be revisited and examined further under the category labeled "Typical Dreams." I will now present additional illustrations to demonstrate that despite their undesirable content, all of these dreams must be interpreted as manifestations of unconscious desires. For the subsequent dream, which was once again narrated to me in order to dissuade me from hastily generalizing the theory of wish fulfillment in dreams, I must express my gratitude not to a patient, but to a knowledgeable jurist within my circle of acquaintance. My source divulges, 'I envision myself strolling in front of my residence, accompanied by a lady.' Adjacent to me stands a sealed carriage, from which a gentleman approaches with confidence as he declares his status as a police officer and requests my compliance in accompanying him. "I kindly request for a period of time to organize my personal matters. Is it conceivable to assume that my desire would be to be apprehended?" "Certainly not," I must concede. Are you aware of the charge for which you were arrested?" "Yes, to my knowledge it is for the crime of infanticide." "Infanticide? However, it is commonly understood that only a mother would be capable of committing this act upon her newborn child." "Indeed, that statement holds true." "[...] And under what circumstances did you experience this dream; what transpired on the evening preceding it?" "I would prefer not to disclose that information; it is a delicate matter." "Nevertheless, it is necessary for me to obtain this knowledge, otherwise we would have to forego the interpretation of the dream." "Very well, then I shall disclose it to you. I did not spend the night at home, rather, I stayed at the residence of a lady who holds great significance in my life. When we awoke in the morning, another occurrence transpired between us. Subsequently, I returned to sleep and envisioned the scenario I have previously described to you." "Is the woman married?" "Indeed." "And do you harbor reservations about her conceiving a child?" "No; such an occurrence could potentially lead to our exposure." "Therefore, do you abstain from engaging in customary sexual intercourse?" "I take precautions to withdraw prior to ejaculation." "May I infer that you employed this method multiple times throughout the night, and that you awakened in the morning uncertain of its success?" "That possibility cannot be dismissed." "Hence, your dream can be interpreted as the realization of a desire. Through its utilization, you ensure the certainty that you have not conceived a child, or, in essence, that you have terminated a life. I am capable of easily illustrating the connecting links. Do you recall our previous discussion concerning the marital distress (Ehenot) and the inconsistency of permitting the practice of sexual intercourse as long as no conception occurs, while penalizing any transgression after the union of ovum

and semen leading to the formation of a fetus? In light of this, we also recalled the medieval dispute regarding the precise moment at which the soul is truly present within the fetus, as the notion of murder becomes permissible only from that juncture onward. Undoubtedly, you are also familiar with the harrowing poem by Lenau, which equates infanticide and the prevention of children on the same level."
"Curiously, I had coincidentally pondered upon Lenau during the afternoon." "Yet again, another manifestation of your dream. Furthermore, I will now proceed to illustrate another instance of wish fulfillment within your dream. You proceed in front of your residence accompanied by the lady on your arm. So, you escort her to your residence, rather than staying the night at her abode, as you currently do. The phenomenon of the fulfillment of desires, which lies at the core of dreams, assumes an unpleasant guise for potentially multiple reasons. In my essay

discussing the etiology of anxiety neuroses, it becomes evident that I consider interrupted coitus as a contributing factor to the development of neurotic apprehension. It would be in line with this concept that if, following repeated cohabitation of the type mentioned, you were to be left in a state of discomfort, which now becomes a contributing factor in the composition of your dream. You also employ this unfavorable state of mind to conceal the wish-fulfillment. Moreover, the issue of infanticide remains unexplained at present. Why is it that this particular crime, which predominantly affects women, has happened to you?" "I must admit to you that I was engaged in such a matter in the past. Due to my own culpability, a woman attempted to shield herself from the repercussions of a connection with me by arranging for termination of a pregnancy. I had no involvement in carrying out the plan, but I was naturally anxious for a long time about the potential discovery of the affair. I comprehend; this memory provided a secondary explanation as to why the assumption that you had executed your task poorly must have caused you distress.

A young physician, upon hearing this dream from my colleague and understanding its implications, evidently felt compelled to emulate it in a dream of his own, employing its mode of thinking to another subject. The day prior, he had submitted a statement regarding his income, which was entirely truthful, as he had minimal amounts to declare. He never would have imagined that an acquaintance of his came from a meeting of the tax commission and informed him that all the other income declarations had passed uncontested, but that his own had aroused general suspicion, and that he would be condemned with a substantial penalty. The dream is an inadequately concealed manifestation of the desire to be recognized as a physician with substantial earnings. It also recounts the tale of the young girl who was cautioned against accepting her suitor due to his volatile nature, which would invariably result in him subjecting her to physical abuse following their union.

The girl's response was as follows: "I desire he would strike me!" Her longing to be wed is so powerful that she includes in the transaction the discomfort commonly associated with matrimony, which is predicted for her, and even elevates it to a wish.

If I categorize the dreams that occur very frequently, which appear

To outright refute my theory, in that they contain the negation of a desire or an event that is certainly undesirable, under the category of "counter wish-dreams," I observe that they can all be attributed to two principles, one of which has not yet been mentioned, although it plays a significant role in the dreams of human beings. One of the factors that give rise to these dreams is the desire for me to appear in an inappropriate manner. These dreams occur frequently during the course of my treatment if the patient demonstrates resistance towards me, and I can confidently predict that I will induce such a dream after I have explained to the patient my theory that the dream is a wish-fulfillment. I may even anticipate this outcome in a dream solely for the purpose of fulfilling the wish that I may appear in the wrong. The final dream I am about to recount, among those that have occurred during the course of treatment, once again exemplifies this phenomenon. A young woman who has faced considerable challenges in order to sustain my treatment, despite the opposition from her relatives and the authorities she consulted, envisions the following scenario: she is prohibited from visiting me at home any longer. She subsequently recalls the commitment I made to provide her with complimentary treatment, if required, and I reply to her, stating, "I am indifferent when it comes to matters of financial consideration."

It is quite challenging in this scenario to adequately demonstrate the realization of a desire, yet in all instances of this nature, there exists a secondary issue, the resolution of which also aids in resolving the initial challenge. From whence does she derive the vocabulary she employs to express my thoughts? Naturally, I have never conveyed such information to her. However, one of her siblings, specifically the sibling with the most significant impact on her, has graciously made this comment about me.

The purpose of the dream is for this brother to maintain his righteousness; moreover, she does not attempt to solely rationalize his actions within the confines of the dream. It serves as her overarching life purpose and the driving force behind her illness.

The alternative perspective that gives rise to opposing dreams is evident to the point where it carries the risk of being overlooked, just as it occurred in my personal experience for a certain period of time. In the sexual composition of many individuals, there exists a masochistic element that has emerged through the transformation of the aggressive, sadistic component into its opposite. Such individuals are commonly referred to as "ideal" masochists, as they derive pleasure not from the physical pain inflicted upon them, but from experiencing humiliation and the chastisement of their soul. It is evident that individuals of this nature can experience opposing wishes and unpleasant dreams, which, nonetheless, serve as wish fulfillment for their masochistic tendencies, providing them with satisfaction. Presented herein is a remarkable vision. A youthful individual who, in earlier years, subjected his elder brother to torment due to his homosexual inclinations, but who has undergone a complete transformation of character, experiences the following dream comprising three parts: (1) He is "insulted" by his brother. (2) Two adults engage in intimate, same-sex interactions. (3) His brother sells the enterprise that the young man had reserved for his own future. He awakens from the aforementioned dream with intense discomfort, yet it is a masochistic wish-dream that could be interpreted as follows: It would serve me right if my brother were to make that sale against my interests, as a punishment for all the torment he has endured at my hands.

I trust that the aforementioned discussion and illustrations presented are satisfactory, unless any further objection arises, to establish the credibility of analyzing even dreams with distressing content as manifestations of fulfilled desires. Furthermore, it is not fortuitous that the act of interpretation always tends to focus on subjects that one prefers to avoid discussing or contemplating. The unpleasant sensation elicited by these dreams is merely equivalent to the aversion that we typically, and often successfully, strive to suppress when it comes to the treatment or discussion of such subjects. This aversion must be overcome by each and every one of us if, despite its unpleasantness, we deem it necessary to address the matter.

However, this unpleasant sensation, which also occurs in dreams, does not negate the presence of a desire; every individual possesses wishes that they would prefer not to disclose to others, which they do not want to acknowledge even to themselves. We are, however, justified in making a connection between the unpleasant nature of these dreams and the phenomenon of dream distortion. Consequently, we can conclude that these dreams are distorted and that the wish-fulfillment within them is concealed until recognition becomes impossible for no other reason than the existence of an aversion, a desire to suppress, in relation to the subject matter of the dream or in relation to the wish that the dream generates. The alteration of dreams, therefore, proves to be an action executed by the censor in actuality. We shall take into consideration all the insights revealed by the analysis of unpleasant dreams if we rephrase our statement in the following manner: The dream represents the fulfillment of a repressed or suppressed desire, albeit disguised.

Currently, there still persist specific types of dreams that contain distressing content, namely dreams of anxiety, the inclusion of which among dreams of desire will encounter minimal acceptance among those who are inexperienced in this matter. However, I can quickly resolve the issue of anxiety dreams. These dreams do not provide a new perspective on the problem of dreaming; rather, they present an opportunity to understand neurotic anxiety in a broader sense. The apparent explication of the fear we encounter during the dream is merely a manifestation of the dream's content. If we subject the content of the dream to analysis, we come to realize that the fear in the dream is not any more justified by the dream content than the fear in a phobia is justified by the idea upon which the phobia relies. For instance, it is indeed possible to accidentally fall out of a window, and it is important to exercise caution when in close proximity to a window. However, it remains inexplicable why the anxiety associated with this specific phobia is so pronounced, and why it persists to a much greater extent than the level warranted by its origin. The identical explanation that pertains to the phobia also applies to the anxiety dream. In both instances, the anxiety is merely tangentially associated with the accompanying idea and originates from an alternate source.

Due to the close association between fear experienced in dreams and fear experienced by individuals with neurosis, it is necessary for me to make reference to the latter when discussing the former. In a brief essay titled 'The Anxiety Neurosis,' I asserted that neurotic fear originates from one's sexual life and corresponds to a redirected libido that has failed to find satisfaction in its intended objects. From this established formula, which has increasingly confirmed its validity, we can derive the inference that the content of anxiety dreams pertains to a sexual nature, wherein the libido associated with said content has been transformed into fear.

[1] To pose for the artist. The quoted passage demonstrates Goethe's inquiry into the nobleman's ability to sit without a backside.

[2] I myself lament the inclusion of such passages derived from the psychopathology of hysteria, which, due

to their fragmented representation and detachment from the subject, lack profound illuminating influence. If these passages have the ability to shed light on the intricate connections between the dream and the psychoneuroses, then they have fulfilled the purpose for which I have introduced them.

Mnemonic Induction Of Lucid Dreams)

The MILD approach incorporates the employment of mnemonic induction to induce states of lucid dreaming. Mnemonic refers to a structured sequence of letters or concepts that assist in the recall of information. When it comes to the phenomenon of lucid dreaming, the technique known as Mnemonic Induction of Lucid Dreams (MILD) is employed to focus our attention on the intent of enhancing dream recall or attaining awareness of one's dreaming state. This objective can be achieved through the repetition of a concise phrase in one's mind prior to falling asleep, such as "I possess consciousness of my state of lucid dreaming" or "I shall retain recollection of my dreams," in order to evoke the desired outcome. This enhances the likelihood of a fortuitous realization that one is experiencing a dream state.

The MILD technique may be executed both during the initial stages of bedtime and in the event of awakening during the nocturnal hours. It can be also be integrated with the Wake Back To Bed technique in a parallel fashion. Additionally, it is advisable to recite the said phrase to oneself periodically throughout the day, as this will enhance its efficacy and increase the likelihood of incorporating it into one's dreams.

PROS:

- Easy to do

CONS:

- Engaging in affirmations repeatedly throughout the day or prior to sleeping can be quite time-consuming.

- To a certain degree, the effectiveness of the message permeating your dreams depends on elements of chance

Wake Initiated Lucid Dreaming, commonly referred to as WILD, is a technique used to induce lucid dreaming.

By employing the Wake-Initiated Lucid Dreaming (WILD) technique, you endeavor to maintain consciousness throughout the entirety of the sleep initiation stage. Throughout this, you have the opportunity to witness the authentic process of drifting into slumber as it unfolds. The most straightforward approach to undertaking the WILD method is to do so immediately after awakening from slumber, as it enables your physical state to swiftly transition back into the REM sleep stage upon resuming sleep. Nonetheless, through gaining experience, one can acquire the ability to elicit lucid dreams using the Wake-Initiation of Lucid Dreams (WILD) technique during the initial stages of nocturnal slumber. This approach may also be referred to as the "mind alert, body at rest" technique.

In order to successfully execute the WILD technique, it is imperative that one achieves a state of utmost bodily relaxation. A method of inducing relaxation in the body involves sequentially contracting and releasing each muscle group individually, commencing from the feet and progressing gradually towards the crown of the head. Devote particular emphasis to your shoulders and the intricate facial muscles, as these regions are susceptible to accumulating substantial tension throughout the day. One may also envision their body gradually imbued with a tinted fluid, simultaneously perceiving the alleviation of tension in each anatomical region as the fluid permeates.

During the process of falling asleep, it is highly likely that you will encounter a phenomenon known as sleep paralysis. As the human body undergoes the process of shutting down, it is observed that the individual's external senses may gradually diminish, and a loss of mobility becomes evident. This mechanism serves as the body's protective measure to restrict the physical manifestation of dream activities during the sleep state. One may encounter sensations such as a reverberation sound or a tingling sensation, a perception of bodily vibrations or the sensation of descending, respiratory issues, and so forth. It should be acknowledged that these steps are executed subconsciously every night during the act of falling asleep, and they are completely inherent and secure, albeit potentially evoking a peculiar sensation. You may potentially encounter auditory hallucinations, wherein you perceive sounds such as a dog barking in your bedroom despite the absence of a dog, or hearing someone summon your name. Once more, kindly bear in mind that these are habitual occurrences that your brain undergoes while transitioning into sleep, and rest assured that they pose no harm. In the event that you discover your physical faculties entirely immobilized, with the exception of your ocular faculties, it is advisable to refrain from becoming distressed. Simply unwind and permit yourself to drift into a peaceful slumber. Alternatively, if you awaken from a dream and experience temporary paralysis, maintain a state of relaxation until you gradually regain command over your bodily movements. It is strongly discouraged to open one's eyes during episodes of sleep paralysis, as the integration of dream hallucinations with the physical environment can occur, leading to the potential manifestation of distressing images such as extraterrestrial beings or spectral beings observing the individual, thereby creating an immensely frightful encounter.

PROS:

- There is no need to rise from the bed for an hour in the morning; instead, one can simply awaken and promptly resume slumber while maintaining conscious awareness.

The degree of dream quality and vividness surpasses that of alternative approaches.

CONS:

- Difficult method

- Sleep paralysis can elicit fear-inducing episodes and give rise to perceptual illusions.

Technique Of Lucid Dreaming

The art of Lucid Dreaming encompasses three fundamental disciplines that necessitate acquisition. They are typically learned in the following sequence, as is commonly practiced.

Dream Recall;

Dream Guidance; Dream Facilitation;

The state of being lucid (i.e. attaining and sustaining clarity).

These are elementary pre-requisites. Despite your decision to refrain from cultivating your practice of Lucid dreaming for occult purposes.

Dream Recall can serve as a technique for enhancing one's conscious perception and recollection of their dreams. Individuals who wake up every morning with the primary intention of forgetting the content of their recent dreaming experiences do not take notice of Lucid Dreamers. The same holds true for those individuals who firmly believe they never experience dreams. It is imperative to cultivate mental discipline in order to enhance one's awareness of personal aspirations. The technique of recalling one's dreams in great detail is an exemplary practice, and dreamers often observe a significant enhancement in their dream memory after a few nights of diligent exercise.

Determining the subject matter of your dream while you are still conscious is known as Directed Dreaming. In a specific episode of "Star Trek: Voyager," Chakotay accomplishes this in a rather straightforward manner, although it is implied that he must have dedicated considerable time to diligently cultivating his psychic abilities in order to attain such a level of proficiency. In actuality, the majority of individuals will reach a stage where we determine the substance of our dreams, albeit the procedure is more intricate than portrayed in a brief television program (nonetheless, it is reasonable to assume that the screenwriters of that episode possessed sound knowledge on the subject). It is imperative to note that targeted Dreaming holds significant importance for individuals who seek to utilize their education for purposes aligned with their personal aspirations.

In the section on Basic language, I have already discussed the concept of Lucidity and its standards. Becoming lucid is relatively uncomplicated as an established technique, yet maintaining lucidity or preventing premature awakening proves to be exceptionally challenging. Therefore, it is imperative for the individual experiencing the dream to carefully consider a range of methodologies that can effectively sustain the state of lucidity. Furthermore, once these methods have been established, the dreamer should also engage in additional practices aimed at optimizing the quality of their lucid experiences. I am presently equipped to initiate a comprehensive educational program that provides clear guidelines for achieving enrollment in the esteemed institution of Lucid Dreaming. Franz Bardon underscores the importance of achieving proficiency in every stage of his magical curriculum before progressing to the next, and consequently, it is discouraged for the dreamer to attempt a subsequent step before ensuring competence in all preceding stages.

Strategies For Achieving Proficiency In Lucid Dreaming

Lucid dreaming is, without a doubt, one of the most remarkable phenomena encountered by individuals. This phenomenon can be attributed to the capacity to engage with one's dreams in a manner akin to interaction during wakefulness. Once an individual attains a state of awareness within their dream, they gain the ability to exert deliberate control over it according to their own volition, unhindered save by the bounds of their imagination.

Developing expertise in this craft requires diligent practice, yet the resulting cultivation promises abundant fascination. In the realm of lucid dreams, one possesses the power to manifest any concept or idea within their cognitive domain, assuming the role of the deity presiding over their personal reality. Acquiring proficiency in lucid dreaming parallels the acquisition of expertise in any athletic pursuit, necessitating unwavering commitment, resolute perseverance, and a methodical methodology.

Lucid dreaming is commonly regarded as one of the most fulfilling abilities one can acquire, as it enables the creation of a personalized reality for a brief duration. The potential for undertaking various tasks and engaging in diverse experiences is boundless. Listed below are various methodologies that individuals can employ in order to enhance the lucidity of their dreams:

Reality checks

Reality checks are a straightforward technique employed in the realm of lucid dreaming to enhance one's level of consciousness and effectively navigate through dream states. A reality assessment is a technique used to determine whether an individual is experiencing a dream state or the actuality of life. The acquisition of proficiency in performing reality checks is an essential initial measure that should be undertaken to facilitate the induction of lucid dreams. The more often you engage in reality checks during waking moments, the higher the likelihood of their efficacy within the realm of dreams. The underlying concept is that one should consistently carry out these evaluations in one's conscious state with sufficient frequency, such that they become integrated into one's dream state as well.

This will facilitate the realization that one is dreaming and consequently attain lucidity. A widely-used method to verify reality involves attempting to press one's finger into the palm of the opposite hand. In actuality, the aforementioned scenario does not transpire, whereas within the realm of dreams, it becomes a possibility. One may also employ the "attempt flight" examination by propelling oneself upward into the atmosphere. If one is alert, it is evident that this will not be feasible; however, if one is in a state of REM sleep, it is conceivable that they may experience the sensation of flying.

In order for reality checks to yield effective results, it is essential to exercise mindfulness and maintain consistency while conducting them. If one desires to prompt oneself to engage in reality checks, one may strategically place succinct reminders throughout their immediate surroundings. The ability to discern between a dream and an awakened state is a prerequisite for engaging in the practice of lucid dreaming. The implementation of reality verification methods will assist you in determining this. Individuals have the liberty to conduct reality checks whenever they recollect, and it is recommended to engage in a minimum of 2 to 3 reality checks simultaneously.

Example:

Respiration: is it possible to obstruct both your nostrils and oral cavity and still engage in inhalation and exhalation?

Is it possible to penetrate a solid surface with a hand?

Leaping: upon engaging in a leap, do you experience a subsequent descent characterized by a floating motion?

Hands: are the skin of your hands appearing normal upon close observation?

Visual Acuity: is your visual acuity heightened or impaired compared to your typical state?

Improving dream recall

The inclusion of dream recall is documented as one of the attributes exhibited by proficient practitioners of lucid dreaming. In order to facilitate lucid dreaming, it is imperative that an individual recollects at least one vivid dream per night, as this enhances one's level of self-awareness. Recalling and retaining memories of your dreams serves as the initial step towards attaining lucidity in your dream experiences.

When commencing the act of recollecting one's dreams, it is advisable to direct attention towards various elements such as specific details, colors, emotions, linguistic expressions, geographical positions, individuals, and so forth. Maintain a dream journal and diligently transcribe your dreams once they are lucid in your cognition. The greater level of dedication you exhibit towards maintaining your dream journal, the higher the probability of achieving lucidity in your dreams.

A dream journal holds significant importance, as it enhances one's ability to remember, intensify the clarity, and retain precise elements of their dreams. When engaging in lucid dreaming, one essentially awakens the mind while the body remains in a state of rest. If one is unable to recall their dreams in the usual manner, it will prove to be even more challenging to rouse oneself from a dream state and retain consciousness. Exerting conscientiousness in recollecting your dreams will have a positive impact on your cognitive functioning during waking hours. There are several measures that individuals can undertake to improve their ability to remember dreams, as outlined in the following points:

Meditation

Keeping a dream journal

Drinking water before sleeping

Getting enough sleep

Allocate dedicated periods for Rapid Eye Movement (REM) sleep

Visualization

Visualization is known to augment the experience of lucid dreaming and it is advisable to engage in this practice while in a state of complete relaxation. When engaging in the process of visualization, one must deliberately cultivate thoughts and images that captivate their interest, in order to establish a trajectory towards the state of lucid dreaming. To achieve flight, it is advised to employ the technique of envisioning oneself airborne, propelled in the desired direction or specific geographical point.

Acquiring the ability to conceptualize images is a crucial aspect of inducing lucid dreams through the waking state. The technique of visualization relies on the power of one's imagination for its efficacy. When engaging in the process of visualization, it is essential to begin by summoning an image within the realm of your mental faculties, maintaining a state of bodily relaxation and closing your ocular faculties. Over time, your cerebral faculties will gently guide you into a slumber, thereby instigating the hypnagogic state, where it is possible to enhance the authenticity of your visualization.

Affirmations

Affirmations consist of concise declarations intended to guide the subconscious mind towards one's desired outcomes. During the nocturnal period, it is advised to engage in the practice of reciting phrases such as "I shall endeavor to acknowledge my state of being in a dream-like realm". This notion will become subtly ingrained in your subconscious, thereby heightening your level of consciousness during periods of dreaming.

By engaging in consistent utilization of affirmations, you will inevitably experience an elevated level of consciousness pertaining to your aspirations, enhanced recollection of dreams, as well as the acquisition of adeptness in exerting control over your dreams. The utilization of affirmations has the potential to amplify your capacity for sustaining a state of cognitive clarity during your dreams. This is due to the fact that these assertions permeate your mind, inducing a modification in your thought patterns, consequently broadening your level of consciousness and command over the content of your dreams.

Example:

I am lucid.

I possess complete mastery over the content and direction of my dreams.

My recollection of my dream is flawless.

I possess vivid recollection of the intricacies of my dreams.

I maintain consistent clarity of mind during moments of dreaming.

Self hypnosis

Self hypnosis is an efficacious method to facilitate the experience of lucid dreaming. Self-induced hypnosis induces a state of profound relaxation that fosters bodily calmness, diminishes the presence of stress-inducing hormones, and directs cognitive attention towards affirming thoughts. Hypnosis can be described as inducing a state of deep relaxation in the brain, resulting in a trance-like state. During the process of self-hypnosis, individuals are able to access their inner voice more prominently, as suggestions are utilized to implant specific thoughts. During the state of hypnosis, each inhalation and exhalation engenders a tranquilizing force.

Process

Assume a comfortable posture and let your eyes naturally shut.

Direct your attention towards alleviating bodily tension.

The initial task entails mentally forming an image of yourself moving along a staircase, while gradually descending further into a profound state of tranquil trance.

Upon reaching the lowest point of the staircase, one initiates the process of self-suggestion, such as affirming the ability to experience lucid dreams and exert control over one's dream state.

Amplifying And Extending The Phenomenon Of Lucid Dreaming

By honing the skills to stabilize dreams, individuals have the ability to convert fleeting moments of clarity into extended and indelible episodes of lucidity. Novice lucid dreamers often struggle with extending the duration of their lucid dreams, as they can easily become enthused by this newfound experience. It is a prevalent tendency that renders them susceptible to awaken with relative ease and experience more abbreviated dream states. Certain seasoned individuals who possess the skill of lucid dreaming also ponder over the methods through which it can be attained.

A considerable number of individuals experience an abrupt awakening from their lucid dreams prior to their anticipated duration. It is undoubtedly disheartening that, subsequent to dedicating considerable time honing the skill of achieving a lucid dream, one inevitably awakens abruptly, thereby terminating the experiential state of lucidity. Fortunately, there exist a plethora of techniques that facilitate novices and even skilled lucid dreamers to avert such untimely awakenings.

On your next occurrence of a lucid dream, kindly consider implementing the following dream techniques in order to enhance your self-awareness promptly. Doing so will facilitate the recall of your lucid dream and expedite your exploration of unfamiliar dream surroundings.

Maintain composure and exhibit a composed demeanor - refrain from raising your voice or engaging in frenzied movement upon the realization that you are in a dream. It is advisable to maintain composure and remain in a state of relaxation.

Gently perform hand rubs - this distinct action will facilitate the activation of your conscious mind, inhibiting any transition to a state of wakefulness. As the dream began to diminish and lose clarity, engage in the action of vigorously rubbing your hands together until you are able to transport yourself back into a vivid scene.

Direct your gaze towards your hands - closely observe and concentrate on them. It will enable you to discern subtle intricacies that are typically absent in a dream. The human body offers the most constant aspects within our dreams, aiding in the establishment of our sense of self. Additionally, directing one's gaze towards the ground within the realm of one's dream can prove beneficial, as it serves as a reliable and fixed point of reference.

To restore instant focus to the scene in your dream, articulate the word "clarity" audibly, thus fulfilling the demand expressed in your dream state. Through exercising control, one can effectively actualize desired outcomes, thereby highlighting the importance of maintaining confidence in one's assertions.

Perform basic arithmetic operations - this will stimulate the analytical region of your mind.

If you have come to the realization that your aspiration is gradually fading in its vibrancy and intricacy, and is slipping from your grasp:

Rotate in a circular motion – this technique will assist in steadying your consciousness. It is an exceptionally efficacious approach for mitigating disruptions and facilitating the generation of novel scenarios. Whilst maintaining a sensation of being in your desired physical form, execute swift and continuous rotations akin to the spinning motion of a top. Commence in an upright or erect posture, execute a pivot around a central axis while extending your arms outward. It holds great importance to encounter and engage with movements in a lucid and vibrant manner. Please persist in rotating while reciting this phrase repeatedly: "The subsequent situation shall manifest as a reverie."

An additional rationale for the potential postponement of such awakening through spinning lies in the observation that the perception of a certain object or phenomenon using one sense leads to a subsequent decrease in the external stimulation of that particular sensory faculty.

Recline rearwards – this notion is similarly founded on the concept that physical motion assists in elevating one's self-consciousness within the realm of dreams.

Adapt to the circumstances - when your aspirations begin to diminish, persist in pursuing your aspirations. Disregard the diminishing state of your aspirations and instead, affirm to yourself with conviction, "the subsequent occurrence shall embody my cherished dream." According to reports, certain individuals have purportedly managed to reestablish contact with their aspirations through the utilization of this methodology.

As you perceive a growing frequency in your lucidity, you may utilize those aforementioned methods and engage in the deliberate extension of your dream state. Initially, it is customary to experience a tendency to lose mental clarity readily as a result of various distractions. Allow me to provide you with supplementary suggestions to address this issue:

Consistently performing reality checks – by developing a greater familiarity with lucidity, you can enhance the ease with which you carry out reality checks. Individuals who are new to this task can engage in it more frequently in order to ensure their cognitive clarity.

Examine your surroundings thoroughly - the greater the level of detail observed, the higher the probability of maintaining coherence of thought. Direct your attention to the objects in your immediate environment, as doing so will facilitate the establishment of stability within your dream.

The efficacy of these techniques may differ amongst individuals. These techniques will assist an individual in regaining their focus prior to its complete loss. These techniques contribute to the improvement of mental clarity and the extension of one's lucid state. Begin by prioritizing the enhancement of your lucidity on a more frequent basis. Derive pleasure from each lucid dream and do not be troubled by it. Over time, the length of your dreams will naturally expand.

Chapter Fourteen: Optimal Timeframe for Lucidity Exploration

Through the phenomenon of lucid dreaming, individuals possess the ability to engage in novel experiences and explore uncharted territories. Fresh opportunities, unexplored horizons, and enhanced psychological wellbeing await those who engage in the practice of lucidity. The practice entails maintaining awareness while in a state of dreaming and eventually gaining mastery over one's own dream experiences.

Attaining the skill of lucid dreaming necessitates dedicating oneself to it with discipline and regularly setting aside an allocated amount of time to practice. These endeavors require mental fortitude, as the cultivation of a resolute determination is imperative in order to reap their advantages. As you increase the frequency of experiencing lucid dreams, your proficiency in voluntarily inducing lucidity will progressively improve. In order to consistently attain this state, it is crucial to be cognizant of your designated time frame for the purpose of achieving lucid dreaming.

Ascertain your Sleep Patterns

The human brain undergoes a sequential pattern during the period of sleep. There exist intervals of wakefulness during which our brain undergoes rejuvenation, alongside phases of profound slumber that invigorate our physical well-being. According to experts, the primary cause for the occurrence of profound sleep at the onset of the night is attributed to the necessity of our bodies to undergo a rejuvenating process, which is typically unattainable during daytime.

Throughout this particular phase, we transition into the Rapid Eye Movement (REM) sleep state. The period during which we are most prone to experiencing dreams.

Based on research findings, there is an increased occurrence of REM sleep during the latter stages of the sleep cycle, particularly in the early hours of the morning. At present, our ability to experience lucid dreams is heightened due to a dearth of deep sleep.

During the act of napping, it is more probable for individuals to rapidly enter the REM sleep phase rather than experiencing deep sleep. As a result, naps are regarded as the optimal period for individuals to have the opportunity to engage in the phenomenon of lucid dreaming.

Rapid Eye Movement (REM) sleep consistently occurs during periods of daytime sleep, affording us the opportunity to experience vivid dreams.

We have been awake for a considerable duration preceding our nap, thereby resulting in a period of heightened mental activity.

During periods of rest, we achieve the state of dreaming at a more expeditious rate as opposed to our usual slumber. Veteran practitioners of lucid dreaming concur that it is frequently observed for them to undergo lucid dreams either at the culmination of the nocturnal period or during a brief period of slumber.

Optimal Timing for Achieving Lucid Dreaming

Owing to your packed schedule, it is likely that you may not have the sufficient time or opportunity to engage in nap-taking. Certain individuals who possess the ability to experience lucid dreams have a proclivity for targeting these dreams during the early hours of the morning. This could potentially accommodate your availability, including weekends. This methodology is alternatively referred to as sleep disruption. It involves intentionally rousing oneself from a typical slumber and subsequently returning to sleep after a brief interval.

Please adhere to your regular sleep schedule and ensure that you set your alarm for approximately ninety minutes prior to your usual awakening hour.

In order to stimulate your rational thinking, it is highly recommended that you engage in a physical activity for a minimum duration of one hour. One could consider the act of analyzing their final dream prior to awakening and searching for any dream signals or alternatively, rising from one's slumber and engaging in the activity of reading. Upon completion of the given task, it is advised to return to a state of rest and consciously contemplate the ability to discern and acknowledge one's current state of dreaming. Engaging in reality checks can facilitate the recognition of one's current dream state.

By consistently applying effort and maintaining a strong sense of determination, it is probable that you will be able to achieve a state of lucidity within a matter of days. After successfully attaining a state of lucid dreaming, it is crucial to recall the methods employed in its realization, including the specific sleeping position upon waking from the dream, as well as the techniques employed to bring about one's awakening. Sleep specialists have posited that specific sleep positions may influence or play a role in an individual's capacity to experience lucid dreaming. Should you desire to partake in the experience of a lucid dream, endeavor to consistently engage in the same preparatory practices prior to retiring for the night, including recreating the sleep posture assumed during your most recent lucid dreaming episode.

After having been an adept lucid dreamer for an extended period, individuals may temporarily experience a complete loss of this ability. Despite their consistent efforts, there are instances where it appears that the mind fails to collaborate. The emotions and feelings that one possesses are instrumental in achieving and maintaining a consistent lucid dreaming experience. Harness the sentiments that arise from your innate thirst for knowledge. Envision the sensation of actualizing the dreams that you yearn to encounter. The acquisition of patience is imperative in order to persist in one's practice. You possess the ability to exert control over your dreams, although it should be noted that this particular methodology is considerably more intricate; consequently, it is advisable to first attempt the fundamental techniques.

Chapter Four: Techniques for Regulating the Phenomenon of Lucid Dreaming

While numerous individuals are actively pursuing the experience of lucid dreams, there exists a subset of individuals who perceive the sensations associated with vivid dreams as rather disconcerting. Should you experience highly disturbing dream episodes, it may be advisable to discontinue the practice of lucid dreaming. There exist various methods through which one can exercise control over the occurrence of lucid dreams and ensure restful evenings.

(a.) Assume a lateral sleeping position
Typically, when one experiences lucid dreaming, it is highly probable that they are in a supine sleeping position. Lucid dreaming entails the occurrence of an extracorporeal experience, whereby one may perceive sensations of levitation, flight, or astral movement. This situation can elicit fear in certain individuals, but it is highly probable that by altering your sleeping position from your back to your side, you are less likely to encounter these sensations.

(b.) Establish a consistent sleep schedule
Individuals who possess the ability to experience lucid dreams tend to have a propensity for lighter sleep and frequently encounter difficulties in achieving a state of deep slumber. They regularly experience multiple cycles of awakening and returning to slumber. Establishing and adhering to a consistent sleep schedule will facilitate

restful sleep and mitigate the occurrence of lucid dreaming. Restore your circadian rhythm by consistently adhering to a fixed bedtime and waking schedule.

(c.) Refrain from consuming alcoholic beverages and caffeinated drinks.
To experience a restorative slumber, it is advised to abstain from consuming alcoholic beverages and caffeinated substances. The consumption of caffeine or alcohol disrupts the sleep cycle, leading to frequent awakenings and an increased likelihood of experiencing vivid dreams. To inhibit the occurrence of lucid dreaming, prioritize consistent and sufficient sleep on a nightly basis.

(d.) Engage in television viewing prior to going to sleep.
Viewing television can induce mental fatigue, thereby diminishing the vividness of one's dreams. This is precisely why it is recommended that one watches television prior to going to bed, serving as a means of diminishing

the likelihood of experiencing lucid dreams.

(e.) Cease devoting attention to the phenomenon of lucid dreams.
If one devotes substantial mental energy towards contemplating lucid dreaming, the likelihood of experiencing this phenomenon is heightened. In order to eliminate the state of lucidity in dreams, it is advisable to completely disengage from the concept.

Chapter Three: The Advantages of Lucid Dreaming

There are innumerable advantages that can be attained from the practice of lucid dreaming. The benefits of lucid dreaming begin by facilitating stress reduction through dream experiences, although lucid dreaming can yield numerous additional tangible advantages in one's personal life. Herein lie a few of the established advantages associated with the practice of lucid dreaming:

Confronting apprehensions - numerous individuals adept in lucid dreaming employ this practice to effectively address their fears or surmount troubling dream experiences. One can configure their lucid dream to address a hypothetical worst-case scenario, thereby gaining the reassurance that they possess the ability to overcome it. One may also utilize their dreams as a mechanism to progressively encounter their apprehensions and ascertain effective strategies to overcome them. As an illustration, should one harbor a fear of unsettling, crawling insects, an individual can deliberately impose upon themselves the confrontation of these creatures within the realm of their dreams, cognizant of their ability to awaken at will. You will soon discover that you are progressively overcoming a significant portion of your apprehension.

Enhance and refine skills and abilities – as per the assertions made by Stephen LaBerge, individuals can effectively refine and enhance their physical skills and abilities through the practice within the realm of lucid dreams. Many surgeons, pilots, martial arts practitioners, and individuals in professions that require precise execution of actions, hone their skills through deliberate practice within the realm of lucid dreaming. This is regarded as one of the most noteworthy advantages of lucid dreaming, for it has the capacity to solidify genuine neural connections in the brain, rendering such activities more inherent and seamlessly integrated into one's daily existence.

Enhancement of imaginative capacities - numerous individuals exhibit exceptional creativity during their lucid dreams, and it is within your capability to deliberately foster creativity as well. A multitude of inventors and painters employ the utilization of lucid dreams as a means to unveil novel concepts that can be translated into practical applications. In addition, musicians have the ability to leverage the phenomenon of lucid dreaming as a means to create genuine musical compositions. Although one may not be engaged in a profession that is primarily driven by creativity, it remains highly captivating to explore the brain's ability to form novel associations on a subconscious plane, a skill that can be effectively applied to enhance one's everyday experiences.

Enhance problem-solving abilities - Many mathematicians and scientists regard the cultivation of problem-solving skills through lucid dreaming as a significant advantage. Within the realm of their dreams, individuals have the capacity to contemplate a particular issue. Due to the altered cognitive processes occurring in the brain, novel associations tend to be formed, surpassing one's previous expectations. This will significantly facilitate the generation of novel methodologies for problem-solving. Lucid dreaming can also be employed as a means to address issues within your interpersonal relationships, wherein you can explore different resolutions and evaluate their potential effectiveness within the realm of your dreams.

Stress alleviation – many individuals who possess the ability to experience lucid dreams regard this as the utmost significant advantage offered by this unique phenomena. In specific moments of heightened stress in an individual's life, having the ability to immerse oneself in a state of lucid dreaming and experience a profoundly tranquil respite without incurring any costs can be an immense advantage. Many people employ lucid dreaming as a means of alleviating stress. They may even manifest their most extravagant desires within the realm of their conscious dreaming.

In addition to the aforementioned benefits, it is worth acknowledging that lucid dreaming encompasses a wider range of advantages, albeit typically emphasized by fellow practitioners of lucid dreaming. The sole means of reaping the advantages associated with lucid dreaming is to make an attempt at practicing it.

Triumphs And Setbacks: Unlocking The Art Of Interpretation

It is well-established that during a state of sound sleep, the physical body assumes a relatively inactive state. However, in order to attain a more profound level of this condition, it is imperative to decelerate the heart rate. I have previously conveyed the manner in which I uncovered this veracity. Additionally, I have discovered a method to deliberately decrease the pulse rate. Engaging in physical activity effectively reduces the heart rate, enhances cognitive focus, induces relaxation, and subsequently alleviates the strain incurred by personal tasks. After retiring for the night, it is advisable to assume a comfortable supine position, preferably on one's back. If the position on your back is intolerable, please assume a resting position on your right side. However, I presume that you are reclining on your back, with your arms extended and resting upon your hands. Initially, inhale deeply. Please briefly suspend respiration, then endeavor to consciously redirect airflow to the upper region of the abdomen, facilitating the ascension of the diaphragm. Please perform this action a total of 6 to 8 repetitions. This action is undertaken in order to alleviate tension in the solar plexus region. In relation to this matter, the guidance provided by Dr. Carrington in his yoga book will prove beneficial. He stresses the significance of experiencing a sense of relaxation in the region of the solar plexus, consciously visualizing its expansion akin to that of a blossoming flower, just below the point where the ribs separate. This sensation requires one's concentrated attention directed towards the solar plexus, thereby facilitating one's ability to attain a state of relaxation. The solar plexus can be likened to an octopus. It serves as the primary nerve network in the body, excluding the brain, and governs the activities of the sympathetic system, digestion, and other involuntary bodily functions. As such, it is advisable to avoid practicing yoga with a full stomach. Alternatively, it could exert undue strain on the solar plexus and cardiac region."

Subsequently, please proceed to gently close your eyes and envisage your presence within your mind's eye. Commencing from the cranial region, contemplate the scalp and endeavor to mobilize it, exerting tension upon the corresponding musculature. Next, contemplate the area of the neck, applying gentle tension and subsequently releasing the tension to alleviate muscle tension. Next, proceed to the upper regions of the hands and place your hands at rest. Tightly curl your hands into fists and then proceed to release the tension, allowing them to loosen. Commencing from the cervical region, gradually descend with deliberation, cognizant of each constituent of the physique in isolation, exerting effort to alternately tense and release the musculature until reaching the extremities, subsequently imposing relaxation upon them as well. Does it resemble the behavior of a feline when she emits purring sounds?

Now direct your attention towards the core, while avoiding any excessive mental effort. In the near future, you will perceive the palpitations in the corresponding region of the thorax. Direct your attention towards his knocks until you perceive and discern them unequivocally.

These are the identical undulations that one senses at the posterior region of the cranium during cognitive projection, while situated within the sphere of the spinal cord's functional domain. These are the sole physical perceptions of the forecast, unless one fails to perceive the pressure exerted by their blanket. The audibility of a heartbeat is maximized when in a lateral position. Nevertheless, this is deemed unfavorable. Once you have acquired the ability to remain motionless and perceive the rhythmic beat, a skill that can typically be acquired through a few experimental encounters, your subsequent objective is to acquire the aptitude to sense and hear pulsations in various regions of the physique, giving concentrated attention to each one. Suppose you are currently situated as directed and perceive the pulsation of a heartbeat. Listen to it carefully.

Kindly direct your attention to the neck area. Are you perceiving the palpitations reverberating in your esophagus? If that is indeed the case, please direct your attention to the cheeks. Here, one can also perceive clear tapping sounds. Direct your attention towards the vertex of your cranium. As you experience a subtle sensation in your head, redirect your attention towards the facial region, proceeding downwards to encompass the neck, chest, and eventually descending further. At present, you are experiencing a pulsating sensation in the upper abdominal region. Please refrain from proceeding to the subsequent section of the body until you have established contact with them. Next, direct your attention towards the lower abdominal region. Here the pulsations are heard very quickly, almost as easily as on the neck. Proceed in a gentle progression towards the hips, subsequently transitioning to the calves and finally concluding with the feet. Subsequently, revert back to tending to the young bovines. Do you perceive any disturbances in them? Please direct your attention to maintaining stability in your pelvic region. And what are your thoughts on this matter? Direct your attention towards the right thigh and disregard the left one. Therefore, the pulsations of the heart can be perceived in any region of the body where one directs his or her attentive concentration. On the occasion that your feet experience coldness, you may attempt to heat them using identical practices.

The perception of rhythmic throbbing in the area surrounding the medulla oblongata corresponds entirely with the sensations experienced by a spectral entity in the identical location (via the astral cord.)

One precaution to bear in mind as we proceed: if you have a frail cardiac condition, it is ill-advised to partake in the phenomenon of projecting the astral body. This is due to the fact that the heart serves as the vital organ sustaining your existence, and during the process of projecting, its functionality may be significantly compromised, thus having direct implications on your overall physical well-being as it relates to respiration. Hence, it poses great peril to undermine the function of an already debilitated cardiac organ. However, rest assured that there is no need for concern unless your heart is significantly affected.

The subsequent course of action involves decelerating the ripple, a task that can be easily accomplished. Astral projection necessitates a regulated and unhurried rhythm of the heartbeat. Direct your attention to this particular organ, where you will conceive the notion of your indivisible consciousness functioning as two distinct entities: one being your sentient mind, and the other being your beating heart. The latter possesses the ability to comprehend the thoughts and desires communicated by the former, and it is indeed not an exaggeration to claim such a notion as being close to reality. Therefore, your thoughts and concentration exemplify an autonomous intellect. As a result, if you intend to decelerate or accelerate the heart rate, envision this cognitive process exerting influence over it. You have most likely attempted to transmit certain thoughts or directives to the subconscious mind, prompting you to question how to ascertain whether these suggestions have indeed persuaded the subconscious mind. However, it is consistent that the clarity of this matter always lies within the realm of one's intuition. Numerous individuals express disheartenment pertaining to the efficacy of their power to influence others following their initial endeavors. They are inclined against reiterating the concept continuously until it becomes ingrained in the subconscious. However, consider this: what would be the consequences if our subconscious mind were to unquestioningly act upon the initial thoughts that entered our consciousness? Imagine that you have chosen to perceive that your cardiac activity has come to a halt and that your cognitive faculties promptly align with this declaration. Fortunately, the subconscious mind proves to be resistant to easy manipulation, though the task of either hastening or decelerating the beating of the heart is not insurmountable.

Allow us to resume from the point of cessation: assume a restful supine position, with arms gracefully extended parallel to the body, while experiencing the pulsation of the heartbeat throughout its entirety. Once more, your attention is directed towards the heart, and should it exhibit an irregular rhythm, I propose an alternative approach wherein you diligently observe the heart rate and engage in the mental tally of its beats. Continue this exercise until your heart rate becomes consistently elevated. Direct your attention solely towards the rhythmic expansion and contraction of your cardiac muscle. Direct your attention to the strikes, mentally tallying each one. After a brief lapse of time, initiate the process of meticulously gauging the cadence at a slightly reduced pace. Consider the notion that the soul is presently exhibiting a decelerated rhythm.

Do not cease your efforts to ascertain whether the heart is amenable to your influence. Continue doing this until you perceive your cardiac rhythm reaching the intended rate. It is challenging to determine the exact rate at which the heart should beat in order to achieve the desired level of physical calmness. As an illustration, the measurement of my heart rate during standard projections indicated a frequency of 42 beats per minute. This type of pulsation is not deemed hazardous; concurrently, it aligns with a profound manifestation of inertness. It is widely acknowledged that during periods of rest, such as sleep, there is a notable deceleration in the pulse rate. Consequently, if my regular daily pulse rate registered at 42 beats, it underwent a substantial decrease during nighttime hours. Differences in heart rate are observed across individuals. You must ascertain your level of passivity. Should you experience a cooling sensation prior to falling asleep, despite your awareness of the room's adequate warmth, or detect a rejuvenating breeze passing through your extremities, this indicates that you have successfully attained the necessary level of passivity. Nevertheless, you ought not to feel uneasy. Strive to cultivate an environment that promotes a sense of equanimity and serenity, allowing you to experience both a sense of composure and physical ease.

Alternatively, if the concept of reducing the heart rate does not appeal to you,

you can also explore modifying the typical extent of inactivity during slumber. In such a scenario, favorable outcomes may even be within your realm of possibility. However, it is important to note that the greater the lack of activity exhibited by the physical body, the higher the likelihood of achieving success. The placement of the relaxation area is primarily influenced by the condition of the physique. A state of profound tranquility combined with exhaustion, causing the spiritual essence to separate from the corporeal form by a distance of two feet. Conversely, should you retire to bed without experiencing any considerable fatigue or exhibiting abundant vitality, you may encounter difficulties in initiating sleep, and even when slumber eventually ensues, the astral body shall only detach from the physical vessel by a minute measure. If one retires to bed in a state of weariness, yet not completely devoid of physical activity, the spectral entity remains at a distance of approximately six inches, contingent upon a variety of confluential elements. As the dream progresses in depth, a spirit tends to ascend progressively. Hence, the majority of estimations occur subsequent to several hours of sleep.

Once you acquire the ability to regulate the heart rate, you will be astonished by the heart's remarkable readiness to comply with your commands. Take for instance this scenario: "Heart, your task is to maintain a steady rhythm of 50 beats per minute until you are instructed otherwise." However, it is advised to refrain from continuously monitoring your heart for an extended period as it may undermine the effectiveness of this suggestion. If you desire to gain control over your heart, it is essential to place trust in its capabilities. To the best of my knowledge, the regulation of the heart is the sole means by which to attain bodily tranquility. Through diligent practice, you actively contribute to the cultivation of "self-awareness," a critical element in the progression of astral projection. It is essential to bear in mind that the convergence of all feasible components contributing to physical passivity must be ensured prior to endeavoring projection.

The singularity of this phenomenon lies in its inherent nature of incapacity for movement while existing within consciousness. I designated this condition as "astral catalepsy" due to the absence of an established term to describe it. To put it succinctly, it should be noted that astral catalepsy may be accompanied by the operation of emotions, both with and without awareness, given that astral catalepsy involves a form of unconscious manipulation.

The sensation of stickiness dissipated, only to be succeeded by an equally unsavoury sensation - a sense of elevation. Given that these events occurred in parallel, my corporeal form, which I initially perceived as being physical but was in fact astral, commenced vibrating rapidly in a vertical motion, despite its complete lack of sensation. I experienced an immense sensation of pressure at the posterior aspect of my cranial region, specifically around the medulla oblongata. The aforementioned pressure was highly evident and manifested through sudden movements, so forceful that they caused my entire body to pulsate. This entire experience appeared as a horrifying ordeal in complete obscurity, as I lacked any awareness or understanding of the events transpiring. Amidst this tumultuous cacophony of unusual sensations - including elevation, oscillations, abrupt shifts in motion, and a pulling sensation in my cranium - I gradually started discerning a selection of sounds that appeared both familiar and remarkably remote. The rumor commenced operations. I made an attempt to relocate, nonetheless, my efforts proved futile, akin to being entrapped within the clutches of an enigmatic and immensely influential guiding entity. Upon the resumption of the auditory faculty, the visual sense commenced functioning. I was astounded when I first began to observe. My astonishment is beyond verbal description.

Offspring of the Devil and Demon

I frequently encounter inquiries regarding the existence of demons residing in hell, patiently awaiting the arrival of individuals who pass in with their astral bodies, only to be overtaken. This belief predominantly originates from the realm of occultism and sorcery, likely tracing its origins back to the very inception of voodoo practices. However, it should be noted that numerous portrayals of this belief are severely misrepresented.

There exist numerous entities inhabiting the lower astral realms, aimlessly navigating without a governing authority or affiliating with more powerful entities for their protection. There is little disparity, as individuals also strategize when venturing into zones of conflict to navigate and safeguard themselves - whether executed by law enforcement, military forces, or the local organized crime syndicates. Even accounts of obsession tend to romanticize the notion that individuals are rendered helpless, unable to resist its grip, and inevitably succumb to its influence.

In every instance, nevertheless, the malevolent entity, akin to a vampire, is compelled to seek permission prior to gaining access to the energetic realm of a human individual. Typically, these approvals are bestowed during elevated states of consciousness or within the realm of dreams. They may also be granted under exigent circumstances, when individuals are willing to relinquish control over every aspect of their lives in order to evade confronting a particular subject matter.

To this point, I have experienced a singular encounter with an entity that could potentially be categorized as a demon as per the principles and beliefs within the realm of occult studies. The course and methodology employed in studying this entity persisted over a span of numerous years, contingent upon its consistent adherence to my energy field. The narrative of this meeting unfolded in the following manner:

Upon completing my transition into my electric form, an unfamiliar sound abruptly reached my auditory senses. It resonated as if a sharp impact or a swift motion of the tongue occurred. I had just been in a state of slumber, indicating that I was either about to dispose of the corpse or had recently returned from doing so. However, I was able to maintain normal levels of attentiveness.

Subsequently, I perceived the sound once more. I reclined upon the edge of the bedside, facing the leftward balcony window, while an unfamiliar sound emanated from a concealed origin situated directly behind me, originating from my place of rest.

Upon diverting my attention to the rear, I swiftly perceived a sensation of an object adorning my person. The experience was displeasing and resembled a substantial parasite that nearly engulfed the entirety of my posterior. Subsequently, I engaged my introspective perception and promptly beheld a significantly voluminous silhouette adjoined to my posterior and oscillating in front of me.

The creature appeared akin to an unadorned ebony gastropod, evoking an immediate impression of sentience, undoubtedly reminiscent of infernal entities or similar beings that perhaps lurk in the shadows, potentially drawing sustenance from human vitality. This facet of my character also responded with apprehension and desired to terminate the encounter. However, I managed to compose myself and express the notion that evading the situation by flight did not resolve the issue since that "demon" appeared indifferent to its perceptibility. "I remain uncertain of its veracity," he remarked, "and I find myself at a loss for a course of action."

What lay concealed beneath the essence of this entity, and from whence did it originate? But I received no further information.

Once more, my anxious disposition surfaced and urged me to vigorously shake this entity or engage in any alternative action in order to banish it, yet my ability to move remained hindered. Furthermore, I was apprehensive that terminating the slumber ritual would result in my awakening and consequently losing sight of this malevolent entity, thereby precluding me from rectifying the issue until a subsequent occasion arises for direct interaction.

This would offer no assistance to anyone. The increasing distinctiveness between my own self and my personality facet grew, prompting a swift deliberation regarding the plausibility of an entity of this nature managing to pierce the barrier on the lower astral plane and potentially exerting a partial control over me. In what manner did he manage to permeate it and to what extent did he exert influence on my thoughts and emotions? To what extent did he occupy my thoughts and deplete my energy on a daily basis?

Presently, a sensation of intense heat encompassed my entire dorsal region, and the discomfort I experienced manifested with increasing intensity. Regrettably, I regained consciousness shortly thereafter in my corporeal form, thus terminating the connection.

The challenge lies in determining the appropriate course of action in this particular scenario. Regrettably, I was unaware as it was my initial interaction with such an entity. To me, this entity was not a demon; rather, it appeared to be a resident of a specific realm within the astral plane. For inexplicable reasons, he had sought my presence. In the subsequent instance of disembodiment, this peculiar entity continued:

Once again, today I found myself indulging in a nap that lasted nearly three hours during the afternoon. In the evening, I retired to my sleeping quarters and directed my attention towards an extra-corporeal encounter. It required a considerable duration for me to unwind, and following approximately 45 minutes, the initial sensations manifested. Once more, a sensation washed over my body, followed by the occurrence of peculiar sounds that momentarily caused a fizzing sensation in my ears. I have finally transitioned from my previous physical form to an alternate embodiment.

I made an attempt to shift my position sideways, yet to my astonishment, this maneuver fell short in separating my consciousness from my corporeal form. Instead, I experienced a mere rotation and found myself remaining in the same spot. Despite the increased speed at which I detach, I still need to engage in further practice. It continues to require a significant amount of time, especially when occasions arise where I may need as long as five minutes.

As I positioned myself in my bedroom, I vocalized with a clear and assertive tone that I was now able to perceive my surroundings. This directive has demonstrated considerable utility in recent occurrences when challenges emerged in perceiving the environment with clarity. Similar to a scene from a cinematic production, the atmosphere gradually became ingrained.

Initially, my vision was confined to a limited area, but subsequently, the broader context became perceptible to me. Now I could discern the location of my surroundings: I found myself situated within a subterranean chamber. I had no comprehension of the means by which I arrived at this location. Adorning the wall were oversized containers and an abundance of clutter, which undoubtedly served no further purpose. I observed, towards my right, the presence of a window that exhibited an intricate wire-mesh design. I resolved to utilize this window as a means of accessing the exterior.

Upon traversing the window, I encountered a formidable opposition. I was unable to achieve sufficient penetration through the window. It had the consistency of chewing gum, impeding my ability to progress. I had encountered issues on a few occasions in the past, wherein I struggled to gain entry through a door or window. Determining it was time to resolve this recurring problem, I took the initiative this time.

Infrequently occurring, yet when it did transpire, it needlessly impeded my progress. Therefore, it became imperative to direct our attention towards this matter.

Upon the occurrence of this issue, two potential explanations presented themselves to me: either my level of consciousness was inadequate, or my psycho-psychic structure rendered me overly dense. However, considering my profound sense of awareness and clarity, it became evident that the latter explanation held true – I was indeed excessively rigid. Regardless of this, it is nonetheless feasible for the second entity to effectively penetrate objects. Therefore, my primary focus was directed towards diminishing my bodily density. After a brief interval, I managed to breach the window; however, my contentment remained unattained.

Upon exiting, I immediately took flight, ascending into the sky to observe the city from an aerial vantage point. Although I found the flight enjoyable, it reminded me of a previous experience in which I encountered gilded creatures within the depths of the underworld. During this expedition, I discerned a weight resting upon my posterior, steadfastly gripping onto my person. I found it intriguing to discover the identity or nature of the person or object in question. Upon the realization of this concept, I immediately sensed a sensation emanating from my back. I ascended into the atmosphere and addressed him: "

I inquired about your desire.

I find it highly intriguing to be in your presence," I discerned the entity whisper, appearing remarkably human, while the luminosity initially struck me as masculine, albeit uncertainty lingered regarding its true nature discerned solely through the faint sound of its voice.

I inquired, "May I know what piques your interest?"

I enjoy visiting and participating in your experiences."

Excuse me, may I inquire about your name? I am interested in knowing at this moment.

Allow me to introduce myself as Mr. Wesselmann."

I inquired about Wesselmann, though my tone carried a discernible touch of humanity in stark contrast to his aloof regard. I pondered the connection between the deceased, who seemingly persisted in trailing closely in my wake.

I hereby instruct you, Mr. Wesselmann, to maintain a respectable distance from me in future encounters." I commanded, causing him to retreat. I fervently desired that this admonition had made a lasting impression, preventing any future encounters with him.

I engaged in prolonged contemplation regarding the true identity of Mr. Wesselmann, perplexed by the enigmatic nature of this individual. When I mentioned the presence of an individual, whoever they may have been, he referred to them as Herr Wesselmann.

This statement was rather entertaining, and I subsequently conducted some investigation the following day; however, my efforts yielded no remarkable findings.

The entity also expressed its desire to be actively involved in my life. During my experiences in an astral state, I occasionally perceived the sensation of a Koala bear gently perching on my back and soaring alongside me.

As I shifted my gaze, his hands came into sight. I observed the presence of three digits gripping firmly onto both my shoulders. This phenomenon was somewhat unnerving, yet simultaneously captivating.

During the course of my investigation, I stumbled upon a chapter within Robert Bruce's renowned publication "Astral Dynamics' wherein an identical occurrence was documented, detailing his encounters with said entity - a text I had hitherto not encountered.

An infrequent occurrence within the out of body experience, estimated to affect only one out of every 200 astral travelers in their lifetime, is the phenomenon known as an astral hitchhiker. This phenomenon is equally likely to occur among both novice and experienced individuals. Upon departing from the corporeal vessel, one may experience a sensation wherein something adheres to the posterior region of one's personage. This entity may exhibit either placid comportment or engage in verbal or auditory displays of intimidation. Furthermore, it manifests a propensity to react when addressed, occasionally giving rise to the impression of being transported by said entity or being personally responsible for its conveyance. It is capable of responding when engaged in conversation, albeit with brief, enigmatic, and occasionally nonsensical replies. Moreover, it may offer reassurance of its assistance while cautioning against placing undue trust in its words.

Frequently, one may observe a rugged countenance, exuding a distinctly masculine appearance, accompanied by vibrant eyes. Should one dare to gaze upon this countenance, it is likely to convey a boisterous manner of reproach or intimidation, leaving the viewer with an overwhelming sense of speechlessness. [...] The general consensus among astral travelers is that these hitchhikers are typically linked to feelings of apprehension. Typically, these manifestations arise when the astral traveler has undergone intense apprehension during an out-of-body encounter. In certain instances, it becomes necessary to make a brief telephone call to the hitchhiker, following which the individual in question abruptly vanishes. The most prudent measure is to exercise mastery over fear and refrain from entertaining its presence in our thoughts, even for the briefest of instances. One's sole focus is directed towards the astral journey while disregarding any thoughts pertaining to him. Assuming you possess the requisite courage, it would be prudent to address this situation by resolutely encountering or challenging it. It would be unadvisable to lend an ear to his statements. He is strongly encouraged to proceed, accompanied by a warning of severe repercussions should he fail to comply. If this approach proves unsuccessful, it may be prudent to fashion a baseball bat with the intention of striking him until he dissipates. It is imperative to repeat this procedure in the event of any subsequent occurrence of an out-of-body experience. If the aforementioned method proves ineffective, or if an individual lacks assertiveness or encounters recurring instances, denying the presence of the phenomenon might be deemed satisfactory, albeit with a prolonged duration [...]. Envision the scenario in which his arms fade away and the remainder of his figure gradually fades into the background. It serves as an alternative when considering the hypothetical scenario of him igniting into flames [...]. Form modification can also be utilized [...] It is advisable to experiment with smaller forms, although larger ones can be considered as well. If one can preserve the physical structure of a wasp or bee, the hitchhiker is frequently dislodged in the course of this procedure [...]. The gradual infiltration of walls or solid structures can also be advantageous [...]. Another concept that can be considered is the act of engaging in astral projection to explore the subsequent religious institution or esoteric group. [...] the act of projecting onto elevated astral planes will propel the individual accompanying to the alteration in dimensions. In the event that all aforementioned approaches prove ineffective, it is advisable to consider availing oneself of the services provided by a reputable and proficient shaman [...]. I have often referred individuals encountering such issues to a shamanic practitioner, and the outcomes have consistently been favorable."

I have personally encountered all of the peculiar sounds mentioned by the author. I perceived a sound of impact emanating from behind me in my transcendental state, provided incoherent responses, and failed to dissipate notwithstanding my explicit appeal for it to do so.

To my astonishment, I discover within this excerpt a reaffirmation of the undeniable presence of the astral realm. It appears that I inadvertently allowed him entry into a professional engagement subsequent to our conflict, and subsequently extended to him a cordial invitation.

During the course of the evening, I engaged in a confrontation with an elusive silhouette under the cover of darkness. He desired to be within the confines of my aura. Amidst the altercation, I found myself pondering the rationale behind our engagement in this particular conflict and questioning its inherent significance. In an impulsive moment, I ceased my resistance and addressed the shadow, suggesting that if it desired to infiltrate me, it should proceed discreetly. Indeed, he subsequently permeated my energetic sphere.

Subsequently, however, I noticed a lack of any discernible alterations in my cognition and emotions, even in mundane situations. Hence, I inferred that it likely constituted an inherent facet of my character, one that I had successfully reintegrated or similar in nature.

It was not until later that the astral hitchhiker came to my mind, and so in the later stages of the events I concluded that this was the astral hitchhiker.

Although I may not have been personally involved, I nevertheless contemplated the matter at hand and reflected upon the potential benefits that could be derived from his actions as a fellow sojourner.

The organism appeared reminiscent of a flea, leaping from one canine to another in search of exhilarating exploits. This topic has captured my interest significantly, prompting a surge of curiosity and research inclination within me.

How does it think? What is the motive? Where is his home? Why does it persistently engage in travel? To what extent is the presence of this being beneficial to me in my journey?

Upon successfully shifting my gaze towards him, his visage greatly evoked a strong resemblance to Gollum, the iconic fictional being featured in the renowned film, "The Lord of the Rings." It exhibited a near absence of fur, possessed an earth-toned brown hue, featured a wide cranium, and sported a substantial oral cavity. Therefore, in all subsequent astral voyages that I undertook, I found myself consistently situated on my posterior. This recurring phenomenon led me to contemplate whether this consistent placement behind me might be interpreted as an energetic manifestation of support.

Therefore, I made the decision to overcome it. To accomplish this, I envisioned employing a flamethrower, which I positioned in close proximity to him, or alternatively, a baseball bat, with which I derided him. However, neither of these approaches proved effective in achieving the desired outcome.

In truth, I must confess that I found it disconcerting that the creature was perched upon my back; however, I also found it quite exhilarating, as it appeared to me as if a young child or a cherished companion was being exposed to a novel realm. It was evidently filled with curiosity and possibly experiencing its initial encounter with the human realm. Hence, it is possible that it had emerged from the abyssal expanses of the celestial wilderness and is now observing in awe the multitude of peculiarities in my realm.

I seldom experienced significant differences upon immersing myself in the unfamiliar realities encountered during my journeys. It perpetually induced immense fascination and exhilaration. What is the rationale behind the potential dissimilarity in the astral body?

For instance, during several dialogues with individuals, I contemplated the possibility of their perception of the ethereal hitchhiker clinging to my person, or the ethereal hitchhiker affixed to the person engaging in conversation? I also pondered upon the ideologies it embraced, its semblance to human beings, whether it assumed the role of a guardian or a ruler.

Did his world have analogous components, where cities or villages were likewise constructed? I found all of these questions to be incredibly intriguing and would have greatly appreciated discovering their answers. Therefore, I made the decision to eliminate him.

Thus, we forged a friendship wherein, during my astral sojourns, he enjoyed unrestricted aerial access, beholding the very sights and sensations that I encountered. I was never spoken to in reference to his presence. It appeared as though he was entirely imperceptible to those around him.

After a significant passage of time, I experienced a sense of uncertainty. Perchance, I surmise, these thoughts were bestowed upon me to portray our blissful state, so as to linger within me and derive sustenance from me, yet my challenges in traversing walls or windows had escalated. However, from my perspective, it appeared that the astral hitchhiker may have caused a decline in my energetic vibrations, thereby resulting in the manifestation of these aforementioned difficulties.

On one hand, he aided me in intensifying my concentration towards astral travel; however, on the other hand, it appeared to possess certain energetic drawbacks. After carefully deliberating, I came to the conclusion to bid farewell to this entity:

During the duration of the meditation, I was in a state of slumber. However, shortly thereafter, I returned to my residence with an inexplicable sensation. I found myself in a state of accuracy within my second physical vessel. Concurrently, I maintained a supine position in my resting abode, within the realm of my well-known sleeping quarters. Shortly afterwards, I was approached by an individual who proceeded to make physical contact with my shoulder, firmly gripping it and engaging in the act of tickling. The hand in question possessed diminutive proportions, resembling that of a child's, yet distinguished by its elongated fingers... There is no other possibility than the presence of the astral hitchhiker.

This epiphany transported me back to my corporeal form. Upon awakening, I noticed the absence of his hand resting on my shoulder. One can solely experience it on the astral realm. As I lay in my bed, I was engulfed by the tranquility of the nocturnal stillness, contemplating potential strategies to extricate myself from his presence.

I sought solace in relaxation and turned to dissociation. From my perspective, the most effective approach to attain the desired set of conditions. My intended desire on this occasion was to eliminate the spiritual entity that had taken up residence within my being. This particular aspiration was harbored within my thoughts and distanced from my consciousness...

After an approximate duration of ten minutes, I positioned myself outside the confines of my bedroom. Initially, I diligently searched the uppermost regions of the structure, ranging from the ceiling to the roof, as I gazed towards the limitless expanse of the firmament above. I had hoped that it would have deterred him. However, in order to ensure my safety, I had to redirect my thoughts. I required a suitable vertical surface or equivalent structure.

Soon after, I found myself in an unfamiliar residential area. At that location, I encountered Zoe, an acquaintance who had participated in a number of my educational sessions focused on the subjects of dreams and astral projection.

She extended her warm salutations upon encountering my presence. What course of action should we take at this point?"

May I suggest attending to the astral entity accompanying us?"

Oh, Mr. Wesselman, the individual who traverses the astral plane," she responded with a chuckle, "Very well, let us make an attempt. That sounds quite enjoyable!"

She became acquainted with the issue through my narratives and consistently referred to him as Vessel with a capital V, as well as astral surfer, as she believed he resembled a ferryman who acted as a conduit and traversed the realms.

Another acquaintance bestowed upon him the designation of a skilled mountaineer, a delightful and entertaining appellative that lent the matter the requisite levity. As a matter of fact, it was quite unsettling to entertain the notion of consistently having a co-pilot in the rear seat during one's astral journeys.

I communicated my intentions to Zoe, following which we collaborated in our search for a robust and substantial barricade. Consequently, we collectively ventured into the subterranean level of a structure situated within this residential vicinity.

In the presence of Zoe, I contemplated the deliberate act of traversing the formidable barrier of a concrete wall at a leisurely pace, with the ultimate objective of dislodging the astral interloper. This tip was sourced from Robert Bruce's literary work titled "Astral Dynamics."

Therefore, I positioned my hands, my head, and my torso in contact with the wall. I cautiously attempted to breach the barrier at a gradual pace. Initially, it did not happen, but after a brief interval, the wall yielded and my body gradually became enveloped by its confines.

I meticulously examined each centimeter. It created the sensation of a viscous, undulating substance. At a certain juncture, I found myself enclosed by masonry, shrouded in darkness, with my sight completely obstructed.

In an instant, a question arose within me regarding my ability to inhale in this particular location. However, I found myself unable to contain a laugh amidst this contemplation. It seemed rather absurd to assume that respiration was a necessity within this second corporeal form. In a deliberate act of provocation, I proceeded to take a profound inhalation, chuckling at the notion that I was capable of breathing in stones.

In such circumstances, it becomes evident repeatedly that the ingrained beliefs from ordinary life persist within these states, despite their lack of validity. Subsequently, I proceeded at a leisurely pace... I experienced a sensation of external pressure on my back, attempting to alleviate the intense force exerted by the wall...

The entire process lasted only a few minutes, culminating in my eventual emergence on the opposite side of the wall. I harbored the expectation that this would prove effective in eliminating the astral hitch hiker.

Upon reaching the opposite side of the wall, I held the optimistic belief that this undertaking had at last rid me of the astral passenger. I might only have the opportunity to verify this again during my upcoming assignment, as of now I no longer sensed his presence. Having attained contentment, I diligently reentered my corporeal vessel.

The ethereal traveler indeed vanished. I persisted in my search, yet I was unable to perceive his presence any longer. However, I did not perceive a distinct alteration within myself; rather, I became capable once more of traversing windows and walls.

However, I observed no significant disparity. At times, I contemplated the extent to which my unwavering stylistic approach had truly been advantageous, as it became evident that a bond had grown between us.

Interacting with such individuals can be quite unsettling, given your lack of familiarity with such interactions. It is imperative that you eliminate the sense of horror and gravity surrounding the issue at hand. Under no circumstances should one panic upon encountering such a entity.

Typically, it is merely intriguing, and the lack of aesthetic appeal does not necessarily correlate to malevolence and devastation to the same extent.

www.ingramcontent.com/pod-product-compliance
Lightning Source LLC
Chambersburg PA
CBHW050029130526
44590CB00042B/2302